# COOKING
## FOR TWO

Suzie Smith

BARNES
& NOBLE
BOOKS
NEW YORK

# Contents

## *Desserts*

# Introduction

One and two person households are becoming increasingly common, yet most recipes are still written to serve four to eight people. *Cooking for Two*, however, is a reflection of contemporary trends and is specifically designed for two servings – you'll never have to divide recipe quantities again.

Perfect for after work or for weekend lunches, the recipes are quick, simple, light and fresh.

In an ideal world we would decide what to cook, then go shopping for the necessary ingredients. The constraints of modern living, however, mean that most of us rarely find time to shop each night for dinner. Because this book uses basic ingredients, you won't have to think that far ahead – you'll be able to choose what to cook *after* you've shopped. A big shop to replenish the pantry and fridge every few weeks should give you the essentials for these recipes.

Although the ingredients aren't exotic, they do rely on quality and freshness, which is necessary to maintain the appeal of these simple recipes. Try your local store for ingredients, as many are becoming more adventurous in what they stock. It may be worth asking the storekeeper to order in certain foods.

None of the ingredients used in these recipes are difficult to source, however substitutes are suggested if you don't have what is listed. Don't be afraid to use something different if you want. In many ways, a recipe is just a suggestion, you are free to interpret it as you would like. The quantities in all the recipes can be varied a little too, depending on how hungry you are. For example, add extra vegetables to a dish or cook more pasta or a larger chicken breast. Be aware that they may take a little longer to cook.

Shop for ingredients you know you like. This way, you can incorporate them into the recipes for your own unique flavor. When shopping, remember also that you are buying for two. Don't buy jumbo packs, and ask to have large fruits and vegetables halved.

The deli and supermarket are good sources of ingredients. More supermarkets now have an international section which offers a wide variety of interesting and storable foods. Make sure you buy the best quality ingredients — olive oil, parmesan, fresh or dried pasta of any shape or form, packaged chicken stock. Scented rices, canned tuna and beans all make a useful basis for a dish, and ham, bacon or prosciutto can be a flavorsome addition.

Fruit and vegetables are not as easy to store for a long time but a few essentials never go astray. Red bell peppers, cucumbers, lemons, parsley, garlic and potatoes are all integral to the recipes in this book and will store in the fridge or pantry for up to a week.

For an accompaniment to your meal, salad greens dressed and sprinkled with grated parmesan or crumbled feta go with just about anything, as does bread and butter and a glass of wine.

For a quick dessert the recipes in this book should provide you with inspiration, but you can also try fresh or canned fruit (in natural juices) with thick cream or yogurt; summer berries with exotic ice creams, drizzled with honey; ice cream and storebought sauces sprinkled with lightly toasted nuts; pears with cheese; and coffee and chocolate.

*Cooking for Two* is full of time saving dishes that require minimal ingredients, preparation, equipment and cleaning — the kind of recipes our busy lives demand.

# *Asparagus with poached egg and basil butter dressing*

***Preparation 5 minutes***
***Cooking time 15 minutes***

**INGREDIENTS**

*2 bunches asparagus, trimmed and cut into 2-inch (5 cm) pieces*
*2 tablespoons butter*
*2 teaspoons olive oil*
*1 teaspoon balsamic vinegar*
*1/4 cup (1/2 oz/15 g) torn basil leaves*
*2 slices prosciutto*
*2 eggs*
*2 bread rolls*
*2 slices cheese*
*freshly ground pepper*
*1/4 cup (1 oz/30 g) shaved parmesan cheese*

**TO MAKE**

1. Cook asparagus in simmering water 1 to 2 minutes. Drain and refresh under cold water.

2. Heat butter in saucepan over medium heat until golden. Add oil, vinegar and basil and set aside.

3. Broil (grill) prosciutto until crisp.

4. Poach eggs in simmering water 2 minutes.

5. Halve bread rolls and top with cheese slices. Sprinkle with pepper and broil (grill) until cheese is melted. Close rolls.

6. Divide asparagus between two plates, top with eggs and pour dressing over. Top with prosciutto and shaved parmesan and serve with warm cheese rolls.

**HINTS & TIPS**

• It really doesn't matter what cheese you use for the warm cheese rolls — Emmental, Swiss, cheddar, whatever you have in the fridge.

asparagus

# *Bean salad with panfried lamb and gremolata*

***Preparation 10 minutes***
***Cooking time 15 minutes***

## INGREDIENTS

*½ cup (2 oz/60 g) fresh broad beans or sliced green beans*
*1 can (14 oz/420 g) cannellini beans, rinsed and drained*
*1 tablespoon lemon juice*
*2 tablespoons olive oil*
*1 large ripe tomato, chopped*
*1 small purple onion, diced*
*2 teaspoons olive oil*
*10 oz (300 g) lamb fillet or leg steaks*
*2 teaspoons grated lemon zest*
*1 tablespoon chopped fresh parsley*
*1 clove garlic, pressed (crushed)*

## TO MAKE

1. Cook broad beans or green beans in boiling water until just tender, 2 to 3 minutes.

2. Combine with drained cannellini beans, lemon juice, olive oil, tomato and onion. Set aside.

3. Heat oil in frying pan and cook lamb over medium-high heat 4 to 5 minutes on each side. Remove and let stand 5 minutes.

4. Slice warm lamb and arrange over bean salad. Combine lemon zest, parsley and garlic, sprinkle over and serve.

## HINTS & TIPS

• Gremolata is a mixture of grated lemon zest, finely chopped parsley and pressed garlic. It works well with the other classic Mediterranean ingredients in this recipe — lamb and beans.
• Use any green beans or peas for the salad.
• Any canned beans will work as a substitute for cannellini beans.

# *Beef stroganoff*

***Preparation 5 minutes***
***Cooking time 15 minutes***

**INGREDIENTS**

*1 tablespoon olive oil*
*½ small onion, sliced*
*3 oz (90 g) mushrooms, sliced*
*10 oz (300 g) beef fillet, cut into thin slices*
*¼ teaspoon cayenne pepper*
*salt and freshly ground pepper*
*½ cup (4 fl oz/125 ml) sour cream*
*½ cup (4 fl oz/125 ml) beef stock*
*8 oz (250 g) thick noodles, cooked, drained and buttered, to serve*
*1 tablespoon chopped fresh parsley, to serve*

**TO MAKE**

1. Heat 2 teaspoons oil in frying pan over medium heat. Add onion and mushrooms and cook, partially covered, 3 to 4 minutes. Set aside.

2. Heat remaining oil over high heat and cook beef 1 to 2 minutes, stirring. Season with cayenne, salt and pepper.

3. Add mushroom mixture, sour cream and stock to beef and place over low heat until heated through, 1 to 2 minutes.

4. Serve stroganoff over noodles, sprinkled with parsley.

---

**HINTS & TIPS**

- Beef fillet is the best cut, as it does not need long cooking to become tender.
- If stock is unavailable, you can substitute water but the flavor won't be quite so good.
- Stroganoff can also be served with boiled new potatoes or rice.

# *Bread salad with tomato and mozzarella*

***Preparation 15 minutes***

## INGREDIENTS

*1/4 loaf Italian-style bread, quartered lengthwise and cut into 1/4-inch (1 cm) pieces*
*2 plum (egg) tomatoes, chopped*
*3 1/2 oz (100 g) mozzarella, sliced*
*1/2 small purple onion, thinly sliced*
*1 teaspoon drained capers*
*1/4 cup (1/2 oz/15 g) basil leaves*
*4 slices prosciutto (optional)*
*1 cooked chicken breast, chopped (optional)*
*small olives, to serve (optional)*
*grated parmesan cheese, to serve (optional)*

*FOR DRESSING*
*2 teaspoons balsamic vinegar*
*2 tablespoons olive oil*
*1/2 teaspoon Dijon mustard*
*1 small clove garlic, minced*
*salt and freshly ground pepper*

## TO MAKE

1. Combine all salad ingredients in bowl.

2. Whisk together all dressing ingredients. Pour over salad and let stand 5 minutes before serving.

## HINTS & TIPS

• Regular fresh mozzarella can be used for this recipe, or try bocconcini (the small white balls of fresh mozzarella that are also known as buffalo mozzarella in some countries).
• You can leave out the chicken and serve the salad as a side dish to any grilled, broiled or panfried meat.
• Microwaved leeks make a simple but delicious accompaniment. Wash 1 small leek and cut into 1/4-inch (1 cm) pieces. Place in covered microwave dish and microwave on high until tender, 4 to 5 minutes. Season to taste with salt and freshly ground pepper, then stir through 2 teaspoons olive oil and serve warm.

# Cheese-stuffed hamburgers

***Preparation 10 minutes***
***Cooking time 25 minutes***

INGREDIENTS
*2 teaspoons olive oil*
*½ onion, finely diced*
*8 oz (250 g) ground (minced) beef*
*1 egg, beaten*
*2 tablespoons finely chopped chives*
*2 tablespoons finely chopped fresh basil*
*salt and freshly ground pepper*
*½ cup (1½ oz/50 g) grated cheddar cheese or crumbled feta*
*2 sun-dried tomatoes, chopped*

TO SERVE
*2 toasted rolls*
*1 tomato*
*1 cucumber, sliced*
*roasted red bell pepper (capsicum) (optional)*
*arugula (rocket)*
*fresh coriander leaves (cilantro)*

TO MAKE
1. Heat oil in frying pan and cook onion over medium heat 5 minutes. Let cool slightly.

2. Combine onion, meat, egg, herbs, salt and pepper. Form into 2 patties 1 inch (2.5 cm) thick. Make a pocket in center of each.

3. Combine cheese and dried tomatoes. Spoon into hamburger pockets and cover with meat. Chargrill, grill or broil at medium heat 5 minutes on each side for rare, 6 to 7 minutes for medium.

4. Serve hamburgers in toasted rolls with salad ingredients.

---

## HINTS & TIPS
- Try adding chopped fresh herbs to either cheese filling.
- Add your choice of condiments to the rolls: ketchup (tomato sauce), mustard or relish.
- Experiment with your mixture of salad ingredients — try sliced baby beet (beetroot) instead of red pepper and coriander.
- For instructions on roasting peppers, see page 80.

# *Chicken breast baked on mushrooms with parsnip puree*

***Preparation 5 minutes***
***Cooking time 40 minutes***

## INGREDIENTS

*2 teaspoons butter*
*2 teaspoons olive oil*
*10 oz (300 g) mushrooms, sliced*
*2 tablespoons chopped scallions (spring onions/shallots)*
*1/4 cup (2 fl oz/60 ml) white wine*
*1/4 cup (2 fl oz/60 ml) whipping (double) cream*
*salt and freshly ground pepper*
*1 whole chicken breast (about 14 oz/420 g)*
*1 teaspoon fresh thyme leaves or 1/2 teaspoon dried*

*FOR PARSNIP PUREE*
*2 parsnips (about 7 oz/210 g), peeled and chopped into 1 1/4-inch (3 cm) pieces*
*2 teaspoons butter*
*1/4 cup (2 fl oz/60 ml) milk or cream*
*salt and freshly ground pepper*

## TO MAKE

1. Heat oven to 350°F (180°C/Gas 4).

2. Heat butter and oil in ovenproof pan with lid and cook mushrooms and scallions over medium heat on stovetop, partially covered, 5 minutes. Stir in wine and cream and bring to boil. Season with salt and pepper.

3. Place chicken over mushrooms and sprinkle with thyme. Cover and bake until chicken is cooked through, 20 to 30 minutes.

4. Meanwhile, boil parsnips until tender. Place in processor with remaining ingredients and puree until smooth.

5. Serve parsnip puree with chicken and mushrooms.

## HINTS & TIPS

- Make the parsnip puree while the chicken is cooking. Let it stand, covered, in a warm place until ready to serve.
- This dish is especially appealing made with several mixed varieties of mushrooms.

# *Chicken with white bean puree and antipasti*

***Preparation 5 minutes***
***Cooking time 20 minutes***

**INGREDIENTS**

*1 tablespoon lemon juice*
*1 tablespoon olive oil*
*13 oz (400 g) chicken tenderloins*
*4 slices prosciutto*
*4 marinated artichoke hearts, to serve*
*black olives, to serve*
*roasted red bell pepper (capsicum), to serve*

*FOR WHITE BEAN PUREE*
*2 tablespoons (1 oz/30 g) butter*
*2 cloves garlic, minced*
*7 oz (210 g) can white beans such as cannellini, drained and rinsed*
*2 tablespoons light cream*
*salt and freshly ground pepper*

**TO MAKE**

1. For bean puree, melt butter in frying pan. Add garlic and beans and cook over medium heat 2 to 3 minutes.

2. Puree bean mixture in food processor with cream and salt and pepper to taste.

3. Combine lemon juice and olive oil. Chargrill, grill or broil chicken tenderloins at medium heat 3 to 4 minutes on each side, brushing with olive oil mixture.

5. Broil or grill prosciutto until crisp.

6. Serve chicken and prosciutto with bean puree, artichokes, olives and roasted peppers.

---

**HINTS & TIPS**

• Serve the juicy chicken pieces and crispy prosciutto with a selection of delicious antipasti bought from the deli. Artichokes, olives and peppers are suggested here, but you could try marinated eggplant (aubergine) and mushrooms.
• The peppers you buy at the deli will probably be marinated in olive oil but you can roast a red pepper yourself and cut it into strips (see page 80).

# Coq au vin

***Preparation 10 minutes***
***Cooking time 30 minutes***

INGREDIENTS

*1 tablespoon olive oil*
*14 oz (420 g) boneless, skinless chicken thigh fillets, cut into 1½-inch (3 cm) pieces*
*½ small leek, sliced*
*1 small carrot, sliced*
*1 celery stalk, sliced*
*3½ oz (100 g) mushrooms*
*1 cup (8 fl oz/250 ml) dry white wine*
*1 cup (8 fl oz/250 ml) chicken stock*
*salt and freshly ground pepper*
*1 tablespoon chopped fresh parsley*
*cooked noodles or rice, to serve*

TO MAKE

1. Heat 2 teaspoons oil in saucepan and brown chicken pieces on all sides over medium heat about 2 to 3 minutes. Remove and set aside.

2. Heat remaining oil. Add leek, carrot, celery and mushrooms and cook over low heat, partially covered, 5 minutes, stirring occasionally.

3. Return chicken to pan with wine and stock. Bring to boil, reduce heat and simmer 15 to 20 minutes.

4. Season to taste with salt and pepper and stir in parsley. Serve with hot noodles or rice.

# *Crab, lime and caper pasta*

***Preparation 5 minutes***
***Cooking time 10–15 minutes***

## INGREDIENTS

*8 oz (250 g) pasta*
*1 tablespoon white wine vinegar*
*2 scallions (spring onions/shallots), chopped*
*½ cup (4 fl oz/125 ml) light (single) cream*
*1 cup (6 oz/180 g) cooked crabmeat*
*grated zest of 1 lime*
*2 tablespoons chopped fresh coriander leaves (cilantro)*
*2 teaspoons drained capers*
*salt and freshly ground pepper*
*chopped fresh coriander leaves (cilantro), for garnish (optional)*

## TO MAKE

1. Cook pasta in large saucepan of boiling salted water until al dente. Drain.

2. Combine vinegar and scallions in saucepan and bring to boil. Boil 1 minute.

3. Add all remaining ingredients except pasta and garnish and simmer 2 minutes or until heated through. Adjust seasoning to taste.

4. Serve over hot pasta, sprinkling with extra coriander if desired.

---

## HINTS & TIPS

• For a change from crab, try a drained small can of tuna or an 8 oz (250 g) white fish fillet, such as perch **(pictured)**. If using fish, first poach the fillet in ½ cup (4 fl oz/125 ml) simmering water for 3 minutes and flake, using two forks to separate the flesh.

# *Dill and lime fishburgers*

***Preparation 15 minutes***
***Cooking time under 10 minutes***

**INGREDIENTS**

*about 7 oz (210 g) boneless fish fillets, such as perch*
*3 scallions (spring onions/shallots), chopped*
*1 tablespoon chopped fresh dill*
*2 teaspoons finely grated lime zest*
*1 tablespoon lime juice*
*salt and freshly ground pepper*
*1 egg, beaten*
*vegetable oil, for cooking*

*FOR DRESSING*
*¼ cup (2 fl oz/60ml) mayonnaise*
*¼ cup (2 fl oz/60ml) sour cream*
*2 teaspoons drained capers*

**TO MAKE**

1. For dressing, combine mayonnaise, sour cream and capers. Refrigerate until ready to serve.

2. Process fish in processor until almost smooth. Stir in scallions, dill, lime zest and juice, salt, pepper and egg. Form into four patties ½ inch (1.5 cm) thick.

3. Heat oil in frying pan and cook patties 2 to 3 minutes each side. Serve hot with dressing.

---

**HINTS & TIPS**

• Serve the patties inside soft rolls with a crisp salad of tomato, avocado, cucumber, lettuce and this special dressing **(pictured)**. Provide additional wedges of lime, if desired.
• Using a nonstick pan makes cooking easier.

# *Feta and couscous salad*

***Preparation 10 minutes***
***Cooking time 5 minutes***

**INGREDIENTS**

*1 cup (6½ oz/200 g) couscous*
*2 cups (16 fl oz/500 ml) boiling water*
*4 oz (125 g) feta cheese, cubed*
*2 tablespoons olive oil*
*1 tablespoon lemon juice*
*½ small purple onion, sliced*
*1 cucumber, sliced*
*1 tablespoon each chopped fresh mint, parsley and dill*
*selection of meats, to serve*
*4 small pita breads, warmed, to serve*
*store-bought hummus, to serve*

**TO MAKE**

1. Place couscous in bowl or saucepan with lid and pour boiling water over. Cover and let stand 5 minutes. Fluff with fork.

2. Gently stir in feta, oil, juice, onion, cucumber and herbs.

3. Serve salad on platter with selection of meats, warm pita bread and hummus.

---

**HINTS & TIPS**

• Serve the salad with a selection of cold cuts from the deli — pastrami, prosciutto and smoked ham, for example.

# *Fried rice with steamed bok choy*

***Preparation 10 minutes***
***Cooking time 15 minutes***

**INGREDIENTS**

*2 teaspoons olive oil*
*1 egg, beaten*
*1 slice bacon, chopped*
*1½ oz (50 g) button mushrooms, sliced*
*3 scallions (spring onions/shallots), cut into 1-inch (2.5 cm) pieces*
*1 clove garlic, minced*
*2 teaspoons finely grated fresh ginger*
*3 cups (about 10 oz/300 g) cooked long-grain rice*
*1 tablespoon soy sauce*
*2 bunches baby bok choy*
*salt and freshly ground pepper*
*extra soy sauce, to serve*

**TO MAKE**

1. Heat 1 teaspoon oil in nonstick frying pan or wok. Add egg and cook over medium heat until top begins to bubble. Gently flip and cook other side 1 to 2 minutes. Roll up, remove and chop. Set aside.

2. Heat remaining oil in frying pan or wok and cook bacon, mushrooms, scallions, garlic and ginger over medium heat 3 to 4 minutes. Add rice and cook 3 to 4 more minutes, stirring. Add soy sauce and chopped omelette.

3. Meanwhile, steam bok choy until tender, about 5 minutes. Season with a little salt and pepper.

4. Serve fried rice with bok choy and extra soy sauce to taste.

---

**HINTS & TIPS**

- Leftover rice works best in stir-fries such as this one.
- A wok is an ideal way of cooking fried rice.
- Steam the bok choy in a steaming basket over simmering water or blanch in a little boiling water until soft.

# Gazpacho

*Preparation 10 minutes*
*Chilling time 20 minutes*

## INGREDIENTS

*1 can (13 oz/400 g) tomatoes, drained*
*1 cup (8 fl oz/250 ml) tomato juice*
*2 teaspoons balsamic or white wine vinegar*
*1 tablespoon olive oil*
*½ red bell pepper (capsicum), seeded and finely chopped*
*½ small purple onion, finely chopped*
*1 small cucumber, finely diced*
*7 oz (210 g) cooked shrimp (prawns), peeled and chopped*
*1 tablespoon chopped fresh parsley*
*½ small avocado, peeled and diced*

## TO MAKE

1. Combine tomatoes, juice, vinegar and oil in food processor and puree until smooth. Chill at least 20 minutes.

2. Stir in remaining ingredients and serve.

SOLÉ
Recorded

# *Grilled chicken salad with sour cream dressing*

***Preparation 10 minutes***
***Cooking time 30 minutes***

**INGREDIENTS**

*6 small new potatoes, halved*
*2 tablespoons olive oil*
*1 whole chicken breast (about 13 oz/400 g)*
*2 slices bacon, chopped*
*2 small tomatoes, chopped*
*5 oz (150 g) baby spinach or arugula (rocket) leaves*
*1 avocado, peeled and chopped*

*FOR DRESSING*

*1 tablespoon white wine vinegar*
*2 tablespoons olive oil*
*2 tablespoons sour cream*
*1 teaspoon Dijon mustard*
*1 clove garlic, minced*
*salt and freshly ground pepper*

**TO MAKE**

1. For dressing, combine all ingredients and whisk until smooth. Set aside.

2. Boil potatoes until tender. Drain and keep warm.

3. Meanwhile, heat 1 tablespoon oil on a barbecue or stovetop grill or in a heavy-based frying pan. Cook chicken breast over medium heat about 5 minutes on each side. Let cool slightly; cut into pieces.

4. Place chicken in large bowl and pour ½ the dressing over.

5. Heat remaining olive oil and fry bacon until crisp. Add to chicken with tomato, spinach and avocado and toss with remaining dressing.

6. Serve with potatoes.

# *Grilled halloumi cheese platter*

***Preparation 10 minutes***
***Cooking time 5 minutes***

## INGREDIENTS

*8 oz (250 g) halloumi cheese, cut into slices ½ inch (1 cm) thick*
*2 teaspoons olive oil*
*freshly ground pepper*
*2 tablespoons lemon juice*
*2 tablespoons store-bought tapenade (olive paste)*
*½ bunch (about 5 oz/150 g) arugula (rocket) leaves*
*2 plum (egg) tomatoes, sliced*
*1 small hothouse (continental) cucumber, sliced*
*½ cup (2 oz/60 g) combined chopped fresh mint and basil leaves*
*4 store-bought dolmades*
*lemon wedges, to serve*
*1 tablespoon olive oil, to serve*

## TO MAKE

1. Brush each side of cheese slices with a little olive oil and sprinkle with pepper. Heat frying pan or barbecue or stovetop grill and cook cheese 2 minutes on each side, sprinkling with lemon juice and additional pepper.

2. Arrange cheese on plate with salad ingredients and drizzle with olive oil.

## HINTS & TIPS

• Halloumi is a Greek cheese that is quite salty. Some varieties come in sealed packages that keep for weeks in the refrigerator, and are handy to have on hand.
• Dolmades are rice-stuffed grape vine leaves that are a popular appetizer in the Mediterranean region.
• The tapenade, dolmades and halloumi are available from delicatessens and Middle Eastern markets — ask for a variety of halloumi that you can grill.

# *Lamb with creamy cannellini beans*

***Preparation 5 minutes***
***Cooking time 20 minutes***

INGREDIENTS

*2 teaspoons olive oil*
*1 clove garlic, minced*
*2 thin slices pancetta, cut into strips*
*1 can (14 oz/420 g) cannellini beans, rinsed and drained*
*6 fresh sage leaves or 1/2 teaspoon dried*
*2 teaspoons fresh thyme leaves or 1 teaspoon dried*
*salt and freshly ground pepper*
*1/4 cup (2 fl oz/60 ml) light (single) cream*
*10 oz (300 g) trimmed lamb chops (cutlets)*
*1/4 cup (1 oz/30 g) shaved parmesan cheese, to serve*

TO MAKE

1. Heat oil in frying pan over medium heat. Add garlic and pancetta and cook 2 to 3 minutes. Add beans and cook 2 to 3 more minutes. Add herbs, salt, pepper and cream and heat through, about 2 minutes.

2. Meanwhile, chargrill, grill or broil lamb 4 to 5 minutes on each side for medium.

3. Serve lamb with beans sprinkled with parmesan.

---

HINTS & TIPS

• Instead of lamb, try grilled tuna steaks — cook them 3 minutes on each side for medium rare.

• A perfect accompaniment is baby spinach salad. For a dressing, combine 3 tablespoons olive oil, 1 tablespoon white wine vinegar, 1 teaspoon Dijon mustard and salt and pepper and whisk well or shake vigorously in a jar.

# *Minted couscous salad with lamb and caramelized onions*

***Preparation 10 minutes***
***Cooking time 35 minutes***

## INGREDIENTS

*1 cup (6½ oz/200 g) couscous*
*2 cups (16 fl oz/500 ml) boiling water*
*2 tablespoons butter*
*salt and freshly ground pepper*
*½ cup (1 oz/30 g) chopped fresh mint*
*1 small cucumber, finely chopped*
*1 tomato, diced*
*2 teaspoons grated lemon zest*
*2 tablespoons olive oil*
*2 onions, sliced*
*10 oz (300 g) lamb fillets*

## TO MAKE

1. Place couscous in bowl and pour boiling water over. Cover and let stand 5 minutes. Fluff with fork, adding 1 tablespoon butter, and salt and pepper to taste. Add mint, cucumber, tomato and lemon zest and set aside.

2. Heat 1 tablespoon oil and remaining butter in shallow pan with lid. Add onions and cook, over medium heat, partially covered, 5 minutes. Uncover and cook until onions are golden and slightly caramelized, about 10 more minutes.

3. Heat remaining oil on barbecue or stovetop grill or in heavy-based frying pan over high heat and cook lamb fillets 3 to 4 minutes on each side for medium-rare. Let rest 5 minutes before slicing.

4. Toss couscous and serve with lamb and caramelized onions.

---

## HINTS & TIPS

- Coriander leaves (cilantro) or basil is good instead of mint.
- If preferred, serve with chicken or firm white-fleshed fish fillets such as snapper.

# Miso soup

***Preparation 10 minutes***
***Cooking time 15 minutes***

## INGREDIENTS

*7 oz (210 g) Asian-style noodles*
*2 tablespoons miso (soy bean paste)*
*5 cups (40 fl oz/1.25 L) boiling water*
*1 chicken breast, cut into small pieces, about 7 oz (210 g)*
*¼ small leek or 3 scallions (spring onions/shallots), cut into strips*
*5 oz (150 g) chopped English spinach leaves*
*1 zucchini (courgette), cut into strips*
*3 button mushrooms, sliced*
*¼ cup (½ oz/15 g) freshly chopped coriander leaves (cilantro) or flat-leaf parsley*

## TO MAKE

1. Cook noodles according to directions. Drain and set aside.

2. Combine miso and water in saucepan and stir over medium heat to dissolve paste.

3. Add remaining ingredients except coriander and simmer over medium heat 10 minutes or until chicken is cooked through.

4. Add cooked noodles and reheat. Serve sprinkled with coriander or parsley.

---

## HINTS & TIPS

- Flavor this soup with just about anything from the fridge — any leftover vegetables can be added.
- Once the paste is dissolved, you can add the remaining soup ingredients at leisure.

# *Moroccan-style chicken, lemon and olive pie*

***Thawing time about 10 minutes***
***Preparation 10 minutes***
***Cooking time 35 minutes***

## INGREDIENTS

*2 teaspoons olive oil*
*1 clove garlic, minced*
*1 small onion, sliced*
*14 oz (420 g) boneless chicken thighs, cut into pieces*
*½ preserved lemon (pith removed), rinsed and chopped*
*½ teaspoon ground cumin*
*1 large tomato, chopped*
*1 zucchini (courgette), sliced*
*½ cup (4 fl oz/125 ml) chicken stock*
*¼ cup (½ oz/15 g) chopped flat-leaf parsley or coriander leaves (cilantro)*
*about 8 Kalamata or other medium-size black olives*
*2 sheets prepared pie pastry*
*1 egg, beaten*

## TO MAKE

1. Heat oven to 350°F (180°C/Gas 4). Heat oil in saucepan over medium heat. Add garlic and onion and cook 5 minutes.

2. Add chicken, lemon, cumin, tomato and zucchini and cook 5 more minutes, stirring occasionally.

3. Add stock and bring to boil. Stir in parsley and olives.

4. Divide mixture between two 12-oz (350 g) ovenproof dishes, 4 to 6 inches (10 to 15 cm) in diameter. Top each with pastry round, trimming it to overlap edges slightly. Pinch pastry edge and cut hole in top. Brush with a little beaten egg.

5. Bake until pastry is golden, about 25 minutes.

---

## HINTS & TIPS

- Preserved lemons are available in jars at Middle Eastern markets. It is the skin that is used to add a unique tangy flavor to dishes. Remove and discard the pith and rinse the skin well.
- You can substitute 1 tablespoon grated lemon zest for the preserved lemon if unavailable.
- Use shortcrust or puff pastry which can be bought frozen and thawed before use.

# *Mushroom soup*

***Preparation 10 minutes***
***Cooking time 15 minutes***

## INGREDIENTS

*1 teaspoon olive oil*
*1 slice bacon, most fat removed, finely chopped*
*3 scallions (spring onions/shallots), chopped*
*7 oz (210 g) mixed mushrooms*
*4 cups (32 fl oz/1 L) chicken stock*
*2 tablespoons chopped fresh parsley*
*salt and freshly ground pepper*
*1 cup (2 oz/60 g) cooked small pasta*
*4 slices thick bread*
*4 slices gruyere cheese*

## TO MAKE

1. Heat oil in saucepan (preferably nonstick) over medium heat. Add bacon, scallions and mushrooms and cook, partially covered, 5 to 10 minutes, stirring occasionally.

2. Add stock and bring to boil.

3. Stir in parsley, salt and pepper to taste, and cooked pasta.

4. Top each slice of bread with piece of cheese and broil (grill) until cheese melts. Serve immediately with hot soup.

## HINTS & TIPS

• Choose any type of mushroom or use a variety — oyster mushrooms, wild mushrooms, large cultivated field mushrooms. Button mushrooms are just as delicious as any.

# Oriental noodle salad

***Preparation 10 minutes***
***Cooking time 15 minutes***

**INGREDIENTS**

*about 12 oz (350 g) Asian-style noodles*
*10 oz (300 g) chicken thigh fillets*
*3 scallions (spring onions/shallots), cut into 1-inch (2.5 cm) strips*
*½ cup (1 oz/30 g) chopped fresh coriander leaves (cilantro)*
*1 cucumber, sliced*
*3 oz (90 g) snow peas (mange tout), blanched and sliced*
*½ red bell pepper (capsicum), seeded and thinly sliced*

FOR THE DRESSING

*½ cup (4 fl oz/125 ml) coconut milk*
*2 teaspoons fish sauce*
*2 teaspoons palm sugar or brown sugar*
*2 teaspoons rice wine or white wine vinegar*
*1 teaspoon finely grated ginger*
*1 small red chili, chopped finely*
*1 clove garlic, minced*

**TO MAKE**

1. For dressing, whisk together all ingredients. Set aside.

2. Cook noodles according to package instructions. Drain and set aside.

3. Meanwhile, grill or broil chicken 4 to 5 minutes each side until cooked through. Let cool slightly. Slice and combine with cooked noodles and remaining ingredients while still warm.

4. Stir through dressing and serve immediately.

---

**HINTS & TIPS**

- This dressing is good over any salad that includes cooked fish or meats, such as peeled shrimp (prawns), salmon pieces or strips of beef.
- Use any sort of Asian-style noodle — these are usually cooked for a few minutes in boiling water.
- If you don't have a really large bowl, you can use a wok to serve the noodle salad.

# *Panfried fish fillets with lemon, garlic, capers and parsley*

***Preparation 5 minutes***
***Cooking time under 10 minutes***

## INGREDIENTS

*1 tablespoon butter*
*1 teaspoon olive oil*
*2 firm, thick white-fleshed fish fillets, such as snapper (about 14 oz/420 g)*
*2 teaspoons grated lemon zest*
*juice of 1/2 lemon*
*1 clove garlic, minced*
*2 teaspoons drained capers*
*1 tablespoon chopped fresh parsley*
*salt and freshly ground pepper*

## TO MAKE

1. Melt butter with oil in frying pan over medium heat. Add fillets and cook 2 to 3 minutes on first side.

2. Turn fish and sprinkle with remaining ingredients. Cook 3 minutes or until just opaque.

3. Serve immediately.

---

## HINTS & TIPS

• Simple accompaniments are all that's needed — steamed or baked new potatoes and green salad or steamed spinach.
• To make crisp baked potatoes for two, you will need 14 oz (420 g) new potatoes, 1 tablespoon olive oil and salt to taste. Preheat oven to 400°F (200°C/Gas 6). Halve potatoes and brush cut sides with oil. Arrange on baking sheet, cut side up. Sprinkle with salt and bake until crisp and golden, about 30 minutes.

# *Parmesan-crusted fish with tomato and basil salad*

***Preparation 15 minutes***
***Cooking time 20 minutes***

## INGREDIENTS

*¾ cup (1½ oz/50 g ) fresh breadcrumbs*
*1 tablespoon cold butter*
*2 tablespoons grated parmesan cheese*
*2 teaspoons toasted pine nuts*
*1 anchovy fillet (optional)*
*1 clove garlic*
*salt and freshly ground pepper*
*10 oz (300 g) firm white fish fillets, such as snapper*

FOR SALAD
*2 teaspoons olive oil*
*2 tomatoes, chopped*
*salt and freshly ground pepper*
*2 tablespoons torn fresh basil leaves*
*1 teaspoon balsamic vinegar*

## TO MAKE

1. Heat oven to 400°F (200°C/Gas 6).

2. To prepare salad, combine oil and tomatoes in bowl. Season with salt and pepper and let stand until ready to serve.

3. Combine all ingredients except fish in food processor and blend until just combined and mixture resembles coarse crumbs. Gently pat mixture over each fillet. Arrange fish on lightly oiled baking sheet. Bake until topping is crisp and golden, 15 to 20 minutes.

4. To serve, sprinkle basil and balsamic vinegar over tomatoes. Spoon onto plates with fish.

---

## HINTS & TIPS

- It is important not to overprocess the coating ingredients as they will stick together.
- The butter needs to be very cold to ensure a coarsely-textured crumb.
- **To make fresh breadcrumbs:** remove crusts from white bread, cut into cubes and process in batches in food processor until crumbed. Day-old bread works best.
- **To toast pine nuts:** place in a heavy-based frying pan on the stove-top or on a baking sheet under a broiler (grill). Spread evenly in a single layer and watch carefully as they take some time to turn golden but will then burn quickly.

# *Pasta with herbs, ham and parmesan*

***Preparation 5 minutes***
***Cooking time 10–15 minutes***

**INGREDIENTS**

*8 oz (250 g) fettuccine*
*1/4 cup (2 fl oz/60 ml) white wine*
*2/3 cup (160 ml) light (single) cream*
*1/4 cup (1/2 oz/15 g) assorted chopped fresh herbs, such as rosemary, thyme, chives, parsley, basil and mint*
*3 1/2 oz (100 g) thinly sliced ham, chopped*
*2 tablespoons grated parmesan cheese*
*salt and freshly ground pepper*

**TO MAKE**

1. Cook pasta in large saucepan of boiling salted water until al dente. Drain.

2. Meanwhile, place wine in saucepan and bring to boil. Boil until reduced by half, 2 to 3 minutes.

3. Stir in cream and return to boil. Reduce heat to simmer.

4. Add herbs and ham and heat through 1 minute.

5. Pour sauce over hot pasta and sprinkle with parmesan. Season with salt and pepper to taste.

---

**HINTS & TIPS**

- You may use prosciutto instead of ham, cut into thin lengths instead of chopped.
- Use all the herb varieties suggested or choose one or two. Note that rosemary and thyme are strongly-flavored herbs.

# *Pasta with smoked trout and lemon zest*

***Preparation 5 minutes***
***Cooking time 15 minutes***

**INGREDIENTS**

*8 oz (250 g) pasta shells*
*1 lemon*
*2 teaspoons olive oil*
*2 tablespoons tarragon vinegar*
*3/4 cup (6 fl oz/180 ml) light (single) cream*
*1/2 cup (60 g/2 oz) fresh peas*
*1/2 side (5 oz/150 g) smoked trout, skin and bones removed*
*salt and freshly ground pepper*

**TO MAKE**

1. Cook pasta in large saucepan of boiling salted water until al dente.

2. Meanwhile, remove rind from lemon with vegetable peeler and cut into thin strips. Heat oil in frying pan and cook lemon rind over medium heat 2 to 3 minutes, stirring, until golden. Drain on paper towels and set aside.

3. Boil vinegar in saucepan until reduced by half. Add cream and peas and simmer 3 to 4 minutes. Add smoked trout and salt and pepper to taste. Simmer 2 minutes more.

4. Serve immediately over drained cooked pasta sprinkled with fried lemon rind.

---

**HINTS & TIPS**

- Smoked trout can be bought by the half-side from most delicatessens and some supermarkets.
- Instead of smoked trout, this dish works just as well with a small drained can of tuna.

# *Pasta with spiced baked meatballs*

***Preparation 15 minutes***
***Cooking time 15 minutes***

**INGREDIENTS**

*10 oz (300 g) ground (minced) beef*
*1/4 cup (1 1/2 oz/40 g) fine dry breadcrumbs*
*2 tablespoons finely chopped pitted (stoned) olives*
*1 clove garlic, pressed (crushed)*
*1/4 teaspoon ground coriander*
*1/4 teaspoon ground cumin*
*1 tablespoon chopped fresh parsley*
*1 teaspoon finely grated lemon zest*
*salt and freshly ground pepper*
*8 oz (250 g) pasta*
*2 1/2 cups (20 fl oz/625 ml) store-bought tomato sauce*
*2 tablespoons finely grated parmesan cheese*
*chopped fresh basil, to garnish*

**TO MAKE**

1. Heat oven to 350°F (180°C/Gas 4). Combine meat, breadcrumbs, olives, garlic, spices, parsley, lemon zest and salt and pepper in bowl.

2. Form into 1/2-inch (2 cm) meatballs. Place on baking sheet and bake 10 to 15 minutes.

3. Meanwhile, cook pasta in large saucepan of boiling salted water until al dente. Drain. Warm tomato sauce.

4. Serve meatballs over hot pasta with tomato sauce. Sprinkle with parmesan and basil.

---

**HINTS & TIPS**

• For tastier meatballs, use a combination of 5 oz (150 g) each ground (minced) beef and veal or pork.
• If making your own fresh tomato sauce for another recipe, it may be worthwhile making a larger quantity and storing some for use in recipes such as this one, especially when tomatoes are in season.

# *Poached salmon salad with soy and ginger dressing*

***Preparation 5 minutes***
***Cooking time 15 minutes***

**INGREDIENTS**

*14 oz (420 g) skinless and boneless salmon steaks*
*3 oz (90 g) sugar snap peas*
*4 asparagus stalks, cut into thirds*
*3½ oz (100 g) snow pea sprouts*
*¼ cup (½ oz/15 g) fresh coriander leaves (cilantro)*
*1 cucumber, thinly sliced*

FOR DRESSING

*2 tablespoons soy sauce*
*2 teaspoons rice vinegar or white wine vinegar*
*2 tablespoons Asian sesame oil*
*1 teaspoon finely grated fresh ginger*

**TO MAKE**

1. Steam salmon, covered, over gently simmering water 10 minutes. Remove and flake into large pieces.

2. Blanch snap peas and asparagus in boiling water 1 minute. Drain and refresh under cold water. Drain well. Mix with remaining ingredients.

3. Whisk together dressing ingredients. Pour over vegetables and toss through.

4. Transfer to serving plates and pile salmon on top.

---

**HINTS & TIPS**

- Use a bamboo steamer or metal cake rack inside a larger saucepan to cook the salmon.
- You can microwave the asparagus and snap peas or place them in the steamer after cooking the salmon.
- If sugar snap peas aren't available, you can substitute snow peas (mange tout).
- Do not overcook the salmon. It is best when only just cooked through.

# *Pork fillets with creamy dill potatoes and applesauce*

***Preparation 5 minutes***
***Cooking time 30 minutes***

**INGREDIENTS**

FOR POTATOES

*7 oz (210 g) new potatoes, halved*
*1/2 cup (4 fl oz/125 ml) chicken stock*
*1/4 cup (2 fl oz/60 ml) sour cream*
*1 tablespoon chopped fresh dill or flat-leaf parsley*
*salt and freshly ground pepper*

FOR PORK

*2 teaspoons olive oil*
*10 oz (300 g) pork fillet*

FOR APPLESAUCE

*1 large green apple, cored and thinly sliced*
*2 tablespoons water*
*2 tablespoons superfine (caster) sugar*
*2 teaspoons white wine vinegar*

**TO MAKE**

1. Cook potatoes in boiling water until tender. Drain and set aside.

2. Bring chicken stock to boil; remove from heat. Add cooked potatoes and let cool slightly. Stir in sour cream and dill. Season to taste.

3. Heat oil in frying pan over medium-high heat. Add pork and cook about 10 minutes, turning. Set aside.

4. Meanwhile, combine all applesauce ingredients in small saucepan and bring to boil. Simmer until apples are soft, about 10 minutes, stirring.

5. Serve sliced pork with potatoes and applesauce.

---

**HINTS & TIPS**

- Commercially prepared apple sauce can be used in this recipe.
- The potatoes can be cooked as an accompaniment to other meats, including the veal steaks on page 94.
- A simple green vegetable, such as steamed spinach **(pictured)**, will round off the meal perfectly.

# *Pumpkin, ricotta and pesto pasta*

***Preparation 10 minutes***
***Cooking time 15 minutes***

## INGREDIENTS

*14 oz (420 g) peeled pumpkin, cut into 1-inch (2.5 cm) cubes*
*1 tablespoon butter*
*2 tablespoons light (single) cream or warm water*
*salt and freshly ground pepper*
*8 oz (250 g) fresh pasta*
*5 oz (150 g) ricotta cheese, in one piece*
*1 teaspoon olive oil*

FOR PESTO
*2 cups (4 oz/125 g) chopped fresh basil*
*1 clove garlic*
*¼ cup (2 fl oz/60 ml) light olive oil*
*¼ cup (1 oz/30 g) finely grated parmesan cheese*
*1 tablespoon pine nuts, toasted*

## TO MAKE

1. To make pesto, blend basil with garlic in food processor until leaves are coarsely chopped. With motor running, add olive oil in steady stream. Add parmesan and pine nuts and process until combined and almost smooth.

2. Steam or boil pumpkin until tender. Mash, adding butter, cream, salt and pepper. Keep warm.

3. Meanwhile, put pasta on to boil.

4. Cut ricotta into slices ½ inch (1 cm) thick and arrange on baking sheet. Brush with a little olive oil and broil (grill) at medium heat 3 minutes on each side. Remove and crumble.

5. Drain pasta. Stir pumpkin through cooked pasta and serve immediately topped with crumbled ricotta and pesto.

## HINTS & TIPS

• You can make your own pesto or use a prepared variety. This recipe makes about 1 cup (8 fl oz/250 ml), which can be stored in the refrigerator for up to 1 week.
• To toast pine nuts, see page 52.
• For this recipe, you need a slice of the ricotta available in delicatessans, not the tub-packed variety.

Pasta.
pasta
pasta

# *Risotto with scallops and greens*

***Preparation 5 minutes***
***Cooking time 30 minutes***

## INGREDIENTS

*1 tablespoon butter*
*1 cup (7 oz/210 g) arborio or short-grain rice*
*1¾ cups (16 fl oz/450 ml) chicken stock*
*pinch of saffron threads (optional)*
*salt and freshly ground pepper*
*2 teaspoons olive oil*
*7 oz (210 g) trimmed scallops*
*½ cup (1 oz/30 g) fresh basil leaves*
*1 bunch arugula (rocket) (about 7 oz/210 g), trimmed and chopped*
*1 tablespoon lemon juice*
*grated lemon zest, to garnish*

## TO MAKE

1. Heat oven to 350°F (180°C/Gas 4). Heat butter in ovenproof dish with lid on stovetop or in oven. Stir in rice and set aside.

2. Bring chicken stock to boil in saucepan. Remove from heat and add saffron. Let stand 2 minutes.

3. Pour hot stock over rice and season with salt and pepper. Bring to boil on stovetop. Cover and bake 20 minutes.

4. Meanwhile, heat oil in frying pan over high heat. Add scallops and cook 2 to 3 minutes, stirring. Add basil, arugula and lemon juice and stir until arugula has wilted, about 1 minute.

5. When rice is cooked, place in bowls and top with scallop mixture. Serve garnished with lemon zest.

---

## HINTS & TIPS

• This risotto uses a different method to that on page 68 but is an equally traditional way of cooking risotto according to some. By cooking it in the oven, it means all the hard work is taken out — no stirring, just waiting. Do not remove the lid as it releases the steam that is cooking the rice.
• If there is a membrane still attached to the white part of the scallop, this should be removed, as should the whiter muscle that may be found on one side. The roe (orange coral) should be left intact if present.

# *Risotto with shrimp, parsley and lemon zest*

***Preparation 5 minutes***
***Cooking time 15 minutes***

**INGREDIENTS**

*3 tablespoons butter*
*3 scallions (spring onions/shallots), chopped*
*1 cup (7 oz/210 g) arborio or short-grain rice*
*3 cups (24 fl oz/750 ml) chicken or fish stock*
*pinch of saffron threads*
*1 tablespoon olive oil*
*10 oz (300 g) uncooked peeled shrimp (prawns), tails left intact, if desired*
*2 teaspoons grated lemon zest*
*1 tablespoon chopped fresh parsley*
*salt and freshly ground pepper*

**TO MAKE**

1. Melt butter in saucepan over medium heat. Add scallions and cook 1 to 2 minutes. Add rice and stir to coat.

2. Meanwhile, bring stock to boil with saffron. Add ½ cup (4 fl oz/125 ml) to rice and cook over medium heat, stirring, until stock is absorbed. Add ½ cup more stock and cook, stirring constantly, until almost all stock is absorbed. Repeat until rice is tender. For the last ½ cup, stir in stock, cover and let stand off heat.

3. Meanwhile, heat oil in frying pan over medium heat. Add shrimp and cook, turning, until tender, about 3 to 4 minutes. Add lemon zest, parsley and salt and pepper to taste.

4. Serve risotto in bowls topped with shrimp.

---

**HINTS & TIPS**

- An arugula (rocket) and parmesan salad makes a perfect accompaniment.
- As an alternative to risotto, serve the shrimp over hot pasta tossed in olive oil.

Basil
Zest
Chives
oregano
dill

# *Sausages with caraway cabbage and mashed potatoes*

***Preparation 5 minutes***
***Cooking time 20 minutes***

## INGREDIENTS

*14 oz (420 g) potatoes, peeled and cut into large chunks*
*1/4 head cabbage (about 8 oz/250 g), sliced*
*2 teaspoons olive oil*
*1/2 teaspoon caraway seeds*
*salt and freshly ground pepper*
*1/4 cup (2 fl oz/60 ml) light (single) cream*
*1/4 cup (2 fl oz/60 ml) milk*
*2 teaspoons butter*
*1 clove garlic, pressed (crushed)*
*2 tablespoons grated parmesan cheese*
*7 oz (210 g) sausages*
*shavings of parmesan cheese, to serve*

## TO MAKE

1. Place potatoes in saucepan and add water to cover. Cover, bring to boil and cook until tender, about 15 minutes.

2. Meanwhile, cook cabbage in 1/4 cup (2 fl oz/60 ml) water over medium heat until tender, about 4 minutes. Drain. Stir in olive oil, caraway seeds and salt and pepper to taste. Return to pan, cover and let stand off heat.

3. Mash potatoes with cream, milk, butter, garlic, parmesan and salt and pepper to taste. Return to pan, cover and set aside.

4. Grill or broil sausages. Serve with potatoes, topped with parmesan shavings, and cabbage.

## HINTS & TIPS

- Start by getting the potatoes under way, as they will wait in a covered pan while you prepare the rest of the meal.
- Buy good quality spicy sausages — beef, lamb or pork — and serve them with a chutney or relish, if desired **(pictured)**.

# *Seared chicken livers with toast and bacon*

***Preparation 5 minutes***
***Cooking time 10 minutes***

## INGREDIENTS

*2 slices bacon, cut in half*
*1 tablespoon butter*
*2 teaspoons olive oil*
*3 scallions (spring onions/shallots), chopped*
*14 oz (420 g) chicken livers, trimmed*
*salt and freshly ground pepper*
*3 fresh sage leaves, sliced*
*2 tablespoons white or red wine vinegar*
*1/4 cup (2 fl oz/60 ml) crème fraîche*
*4 thick slices bread, toasted and buttered*

## TO MAKE

1. Broil (grill) bacon.

2. Meanwhile, heat butter and oil in frying pan. Add scallions and cook over medium heat 3 minutes. Remove with slotted spoon and set aside.

3. Reheat pan and cook livers over medium-high heat 5 minutes, turning occasionally. Sprinkle with salt, pepper and sage. Remove and set aside.

4. Add vinegar and deglaze pan by cooking over high heat, stirring up any remaining brown bits. Stir in crème fraîche and boil 1 minute. Return scallions and livers to pan and reheat 1 minute.

5. Serve livers on buttered toast with bacon.

---

## HINTS & TIPS

- This light meal would be finished off perfectly with a simple green salad.
- If crème fraîche cannot be found, sour cream can be substituted.

MINERAL
WATER

# *Seared tuna steaks with Mexican salsa*

***Preparation 10 minutes***
***Cooking time under 10 minutes***

**INGREDIENTS**
*1 lb (500 g) tuna steaks*
*1 tablespoon olive oil*
*juice of 1/2 lime*
*salt and freshly ground pepper*

FOR SALSA
*1 large tomato, chopped*
*1 small purple onion, finely chopped*
*1 avocado, chopped*
*1 small chili, finely chopped, or more to taste*
*1/4 cup coriander leaves (cilantro), chopped*
*1/2 small red bell pepper (capsicum), chopped*
*2 tablespoons olive oil*
*juice of 1/2 lime*
*salt and freshly ground pepper*
*lime wedges, to garnish*

**TO MAKE**
1. Brush tuna steaks with oil. Heat grill or heavy-bottomed frying pan and sear tuna over high heat 2 to 3 minutes on each side, depending on how rare you want it. Test by gently cutting into the middle.

2. Combine all salsa ingredients.

3. Squeeze lime juice over tuna steaks and season with salt and pepper. Serve with salsa and lime wedges.

# Smoked chicken and pumpkin soup

***Preparation 10 minutes***
***Cooking time 35 minutes***

## INGREDIENTS

*1 tablespoon olive oil*
*1 small onion, finely chopped*
*grated zest of 1 lemon or 1-inch (2.5 cm) piece lemongrass, finely chopped*
*3 fresh coriander roots, chopped (optional)*
*1 clove garlic, minced*
*1 teaspoon grated fresh ginger*
*1 lb (450 g) peeled pumpkin, cut into 1-inch (2.5 cm) cubes*
*3 cups (24 fl oz/750 ml) chicken stock*
*5 oz (150 g) smoked chicken breast, cut into pieces*
*chopped scallions (spring onions/shallots) or fresh coriander leaves (cilantro), for garnish*

## TO MAKE

1. Heat oil in saucepan over low heat. Add onion, lemon zest, coriander roots, garlic and ginger and cook, stirring, 3 to 4 minutes.

2. Add pumpkin and cook, stirring, 2 to 3 minutes.

3. Add stock, bring to boil and simmer until pumpkin is tender, about 15 minutes. Let cool slightly.

4. Puree mixture in blender or food processor. Return to saucepan, add chicken and heat through.

5. Serve garnished with scallions or coriander.

---

## HINTS & TIPS

• This recipe makes good use of the fresh coriander (cilantro) you can buy in bunches; the roots can be used to add flavor. Don't use the "hairy" part of the root — just the fleshy end of the stalks.
• Smoked chicken can be bought at delicatessens.
• Cutting the pumpkin into smaller pieces makes cooking quicker.

Yum!

# *Smoked trout pâté*

***Preparation 10 minutes***

## INGREDIENTS

*1/2 side smoked trout (5 oz/150 g), skin and bones removed*
*2 teaspoons lime juice*
*1 teaspoon grated lime zest*
*1 tablespoon chopped fresh dill, parsley or coriander leaves (cilantro)*
*1/4 cup (3 oz/90 g) soft cream cheese*
*2 teaspoons chopped drained capers*
*freshly ground pepper*

*TO SERVE*
*2 hard-cooked (boiled) eggs*
*baby cornichons*
*1/2 red bell pepper (capsicum), roasted then seeded, peeled and sliced*
*toasted rye bread*
*salad greens*
*lime wedges*

## TO MAKE

1. Combine trout, lime juice and zest, herb and cream cheese in food processor and blend until smooth.

2. Add capers and ground pepper and process until just combined.

3. Serve pâté with eggs, cornichons, roasted red pepper, rye toast and salad greens, with lime wedges on the side.

## HINTS & TIPS

• This recipe is suitable to use as an appetizer with crackers or toasted rye bread pieces or as a light meal with salad, eggs, cornichons and roasted pepper. The final preparation time and effort will depend on how you choose to serve it.
• Pâté can be served chilled or at room temperature, and will last 2 to 3 days if kept covered in the refrigerator.
• Smoked trout is available by the half-side in most delis and some supermarkets.
• For instructions on roasting peppers, see page 80.

# *Spaghetti with roasted pepper and anchovy sauce*

***Preparation 10 – 35 minutes***
***Cooking time 15 minutes***

## INGREDIENTS

*8 oz (250 g) spaghetti*
*1/3 cup (3 fl oz/90 ml) virgin olive oil*
*3 tablespoons finely chopped canned anchovies*
*2 cloves garlic, minced*
*2 tablespoons finely chopped fresh parsley*
*1 red bell pepper (capsicum), roasted, seeded, peeled and cut into strips*
*freshly ground pepper*
*2 tablespoons finely grated parmesan cheese*
*finely chopped lemon zest, to garnish*
*chopped fresh basil or parsley, to garnish*

## TO MAKE

1. Cook spaghetti in large saucepan of boiling salted water until al dente. Drain.

2. Meanwhile, warm olive oil in frying pan. Add anchovies and cook over low heat until anchovies have dissolved and combined with oil.

3. Add garlic and cook over medium heat 1 minute. Add parsley, roasted bell pepper and ground pepper and cook 1 minute.

4. Stir sauce through hot spaghetti. Serve with parmesan, lemon zest and chopped herbs.

## HINTS & TIPS

- Serve pasta with pieces of warmed Italian bread, with lemon wedges on the side.
- **To roast peppers:** There are a number of methods. You can place a whole pepper directly on an oven rack and bake in a preheated 450°F (230°C/Gas 7) oven for about 20 to 30 minutes, or use a cooking fork to hold the pepper over a gas flame for about 5 to 10 minutes. Alternatively, the pepper can be cooked whole or halved under a hot broiler (grill) for about 5 to 15 minutes. Peppers are done when the skin is blackened and blistered; whole peppers should be turned frequently during cooking. Peel off skin — do not rinse. Remove core, seeds and membrane.

# *Spinach tart*

***Preparation 10 minutes***
***Cooking time 15 – 35 minutes***

**INGREDIENTS**

*2 teaspoons olive oil*
*4 scallions (spring onions/shallots), chopped*
*1 slice bacon, chopped*
*1 clove garlic, minced*
*2 cups (9 oz/280 g) cooked, drained English spinach*
*½ cup (1 oz/30 g) chopped fresh basil*
*5 oz (150 g) fresh ricotta cheese*
*3 oz (90 g) feta cheese, crumbled*
*2 tablespoons grated parmesan cheese*
*2 eggs*
*1 cup (8 fl oz/250 ml) milk*
*salt and freshly ground pepper*

**TO MAKE**

1. Heat oil in frying pan over medium heat. Add scallions, bacon and garlic and cook 5 minutes.

2. Heat oven to 350°F (180°C/Gas 4) if you will be baking the tart (it can also be microwaved).

3. Transfer bacon mixture to bowl and stir in spinach, basil and cheeses. Place in microwave-proof or ovenproof pie dish. Combine eggs and milk and pour over. Season with salt and pepper.

4. Bake 30 minutes or microwave on high until set, 10 to 15 minutes.

5. Serve warm, cut into wedges.

# *Steak sandwiches with cream cheese and red pepper spread*

***Preparation 5 minutes***
***Cooking time 20 minutes***

**INGREDIENTS**

*1 tablespoon butter*
*2 teaspoons olive oil*
*1 onion, thinly sliced*
*½ red bell pepper (capsicum), seeded and thinly sliced*
*1 teaspoon balsamic vinegar*
*2 teaspoons shredded fresh basil (optional)*
*salt and freshly ground pepper*
*2 to 4 club steaks or minute steaks (8 to 10 oz/250 to 300 g)*
*slices of thick Italian-style bread, to serve*
*sliced tomato and arugula (rocket), to serve*

FOR SPREAD

*½ red bell pepper (capsicum), roasted (see page 80) then seeded and peeled*
*3 tablespoons soft cream cheese*
*2 teaspoons butter*
*½ teaspoon paprika*
*½ teaspoon crushed caraway seeds (optional)*

**TO MAKE**

1. Heat butter and oil in frying pan over medium heat. Add onion and red pepper and cook 7 to 10 minutes. Add vinegar and cook another 2 to 3 minutes. Stir in basil and season with salt and pepper. Remove mixture from pan and set aside.

2. Add steaks to pan and cook over high heat 1 minute on each side.

3. For spread, combine all ingredients in food processor and blend until smooth.

4. Spread bread with cream cheese mixture, then fill sandwiches with steaks, tomato and arugula.

---

**HINTS & TIPS**

- The number of steaks will depend on their size. Make sure they are thin; if not, gently pound them.
- Cook an extra minute for a well-cooked steak.

# *Steak with garlic butter and red pepper relish*

***Preparation 5 minutes***
***Cooking time 20 minutes***

**INGREDIENTS**

*2 beef steaks (your choice of cut), about 9 to 13 oz (300 to 400 g)*

*FOR GARLIC BUTTER*
*2 cloves garlic, pressed (crushed)*
*1 anchovy fillet (optional)*
*3 tablespoons butter, softened*

*FOR RELISH*
*1 tablespoon olive oil*
*1 red bell pepper (capsicum), seeded and thinly sliced*
*1/2 teaspoon balsamic vinegar*

**TO MAKE**

1. For garlic butter, stir garlic and anchovy into softened butter. Pat into small dish and refrigerate until ready to serve.

2. To prepare relish, heat oil in frying pan over medium-low heat. Add pepper and cook, partially covered, 10 minutes. Stir in vinegar and cook 10 more minutes, uncovered.

3. Grill or broil steak until cooked as desired. Serve with garlic butter and relish.

---

**HINTS & TIPS**

- Serve with baked potatoes and salad. The crunchy new potatoes on page 50 are a perfect accompaniment.
- The relish takes the most time to prepare; store-bought relishes and chutneys are an alternative.

# *Steak with Mediterranean vegetables and aïoli*

***Preparation 10 minutes***
***Cooking time 25 minutes***

## INGREDIENTS

*1 small eggplant (aubergine), thinly sliced*
*2 plum (egg) tomatoes, halved*
*1 small purple onion, quartered*
*½ red bell pepper (capsicum)*
*2 tablespoons olive oil*
*1 lb (500 g) sirloin steak, 1¼ inch (3 cm) thick*
*1 tablespoon lemon juice*
*salt and freshly ground pepper*
*basil leaves, to garnish*

*FOR AÏOLI*

*¼ cup (2 fl oz/60 ml) whole-egg mayonnaise*
*2 tablespoons sour cream or crème fraîche*
*2 cloves garlic, pressed (crushed)*
*1 teaspoon finely grated lemon zest*

## TO MAKE

1. Combine all aïoli ingredients and let stand.

2. Brush eggplant slices, tomato halves, onion quarters and whole red pepper with olive oil and place on baking sheet. Grill or broil 10 to 15 minutes, turning eggplant, onion and whole pepper after 5 to 7 minutes. Set aside.

3. Grill or broil steak at medium-high heat 7 to 10 minutes on each side for medium, brushing with a little lemon juice while cooking. Season with salt and pepper.

4. Peel, seed and slice roasted red pepper.

5. Serve steak with vegetables and aïoli.

## HINTS & TIPS

- Everything can be cooked under the same broiler or on the same grill.
- If you wish, a spoonful of pesto and a handful of black olives make a colorful accompaniment.

# *Tortilla chips with guacamole*

***Preparation 15 minutes***

**INGREDIENTS**

FOR GUACAMOLE

*1 ripe avocado*
*2 teaspoons lime or lemon juice*
*1 tablespoon finely diced onion*
*1/4 teaspoon ground cumin*
*1 small red chili, finely chopped*
*2 tablespoons finely chopped fresh coriander leaves (cilantro)*
*1 small tomato, chopped*

TO SERVE

*12 oz (375 g) corn tortilla chips, warmed*
*1/2 barbecued chicken, skin removed, shredded*
*1/4 head lettuce, finely shredded*
*1 large tomato, chopped*
*3 oz (90 g) fresh Mexican cheese, crumbled*
*prepared salsa, store-bought or home-made (see page 74)*

**TO MAKE**

1. Heat oven to 300°F (150°C/Gas 4). Place tortilla chips on baking sheet and warm in oven, about 10 minutes.

2. For guacamole, mash avocado and stir in remaining ingredients.

3. Serve warmed chips piled with guacamole, shredded chicken, lettuce, tomato, cheese and salsa.

---

**HINTS & TIPS**

- Instead of tortilla chips, use 4 to 6 warmed taco shells or corn or flour tortillas. Warm tortillas according to package directions — usually by turning with tongs in a hot ungreased frying pan 30 seconds on each side.
- Feta cheese can be used in place of Mexican cheese for an unexpected variation.
- Note that guacamole cannot be made in advance as avocado turns brown quickly.

# *Veal steaks with spinach and mozzarella*

***Preparation 5 minutes***
***Cooking time 20 – 25 minutes***

## INGREDIENTS

*1 tablespoon butter*
*1 tablespoon olive oil*
*½ small purple onion, sliced*
*7 oz (200 g) fresh English spinach leaves*
*2 anchovy fillets*
*1 tablespoon dried currants*
*1 tablespoon chopped fresh parsley*
*10 oz (300 g) veal leg steaks*
*¼ cup (2 fl oz/60 ml) white wine*
*salt and freshly ground pepper*
*5 oz (150 g) fresh mozzarella, sliced*

## TO MAKE

1. Heat oven to 350°F (180°C/Gas 4).

2. Heat butter and 2 teaspoons olive oil in ovenproof frying pan. Add onion and cook 2 minutes over medium heat. Add spinach, anchovies and currants and cook until spinach has wilted, 2 to 3 more minutes. Stir in parsley. Remove from pan and set aside.

3. Heat remaining oil in pan over high heat and cook veal steaks 2 minutes on each side. Pour wine over and cook over medium heat 1 more minute.

4. Pile spinach mixture on each steak, season with salt and pepper and top with cheese slices. Bake 10 minutes or until cheese has melted, or broil (grill) at medium heat 3 to 4 minutes.

---

## HINTS & TIPS

- Instead of veal, you can use beef minute steaks or chicken breasts.
- Serve with steamed new potatoes or rice.

# *Veal steaks with sun-dried tomato salsa*

***Preparation 10 minutes***
***Cooking time 20 minutes***

**INGREDIENTS**

*2 teaspoons chopped fresh rosemary or 1 teaspoon dried*
*salt and freshly ground pepper*
*2 tablespoons finely grated parmesan cheese*
*½ cup (about 1½ oz/50 g) fine dry breadcrumbs*
*2 to 4 veal leg steaks (about 10 to 13 oz/300 to 400 g), gently pounded*
*1 egg, beaten*
*1 tablespoon olive oil*

FOR TOMATO SALSA

*2 ripe tomatoes, diced*
*2 sun-dried tomatoes, chopped*
*2 teaspoons oil from sun-dried tomatoes*
*1 teaspoon red wine vinegar*
*salt and freshly ground pepper*

FOR MASHED POTATOES

*13 oz (400 g) potatoes*
*¼ cup (2 fl oz/60 ml) light (single) cream*
*1 tablespoon butter*
*1 clove garlic, pressed (crushed)*

**TO MAKE**

1. For salsa, combine all ingredients and let stand.

2. Boil potatoes until tender. Drain, return to pan and cover to keep warm.

3. Meanwhile, combine rosemary, salt and pepper, parmesan and breadcrumbs and spread over plate. Dip each veal steak on both sides in egg, then breadcrumb mixture.

4. Heat oil in frying pan over medium heat and cook veal 3 to 4 minutes on each side.

5. Mash potatoes, stirring in remaining ingredients.

6. Spoon salsa over veal and serve with potatoes.

---

**HINTS & TIPS**

- Most frying pans will perfectly fit 2 schnitzels so you can cook the meat in one batch.
- Use store-bought salsa if desired.
- A green salad is the only accompaniment that is needed.

# *Warm lentil salad*

***Preparation 10 minutes***
***Cooking time 10 minutes***

## INGREDIENTS

*2 teaspoons olive oil*
*2 teaspoons butter*
*1 small carrot, chopped*
*1 celery stalk, chopped*
*1 small onion, chopped*
*1 can (14 oz/420 g) lentils, drained*
*1/4 cup (2 fl oz/60 ml) chicken stock*
*1 tablespoon chopped fresh parsley*
*10 oz (300 g) lamb fillets*
*1/4 cup (2 fl oz/60 ml) sour cream or crème fraîche*
*1 tablespoon prepared horseradish*
*flat-leaf parsley, to garnish*

## TO MAKE

1. Heat oil and butter in saucepan. Add carrot, celery and onion and cook over medium heat, partially covered, 5 minutes. Add lentils and stock and bring to boil. Simmer 2 to 3 minutes. Stir in parsley.

2. Meanwhile, grill or broil lamb at medium heat until cooked through, 3 to 4 minutes on each side.

3. Combine sour cream and horseradish. Serve with meat and lentils, garnished with parsley.

---

## HINTS & TIPS

- Serve lentils with chicken or salmon instead of lamb. Grill or broil 2 chicken breasts (about 14 oz/420 g) for 5 minutes each side, or 14 oz (420 g) salmon steaks for 3 minutes each side.
- You can substitute another canned bean, such as haricots or cannellini
- Use 1 cup dried lentils, soaked in 4 cups water for 3 to 4 hours or overnight.

# Baked bananas

***Preparation 5 minutes***
***Cooking time 15 minutes***

## INGREDIENTS

*2 bananas, peeled and sliced*
*1/4 cup (2 1/2 oz/75 g) lightly packed brown sugar*
*2 tablespoons unsalted butter*
*1 tablespoon shredded coconut*
*2 tablespoons dark rum*
*ice cream, to serve*

## TO MAKE

1. Heat oven to 350°F (180°C/Gas 4).

2. Place bananas in small ovenproof dish. Sprinkle with sugar and dot with butter. Sprinkle with coconut.

3. Bake until bananas are soft and coconut is golden brown, 10 to 15 minutes. Pour rum over, gently stirring through. Serve bananas warm over ice cream.

# *Fresh berries in lemon syrup*

***Preparation and cooking time***
***10 minutes***

## INGREDIENTS

*1/4 cup (2 1/2 oz/75 g) superfine (caster) sugar*
*1/4 cup (2 fl oz/60 ml) water*
*2 tablespoons lemon juice*
*1 1/2 cups (about 8 oz/250 g) berries, such as raspberries, strawberries, blueberries and/or blackberries*
*whipping (double) cream or ice cream, to serve*

## TO MAKE

1. Combine sugar, water and lemon juice in small saucepan and stir over low heat to dissolve sugar. Bring to boil, reduce heat and simmer 2 minutes.

2. Remove syrup from heat and stir through berries. Let stand 3 to 4 minutes so berries become slightly warm and soften.

3. Serve while still warm with cream or ice cream.

## HINTS & TIPS

- You can use mixed berries or just a single variety.
- Substitute lime juice for lemon.

# Hot caramel sauce

***Preparation and cooking time***
***10 minutes***

## INGREDIENTS

*1/4 cup (2 1/2 oz/75 g) lightly packed brown sugar*
*1/4 cup (2 fl oz/60 ml) whipping (double) cream*
*3 tablespoons unsalted butter*

## TO MAKE

1. Combine all ingredients in small saucepan and stir over low heat to dissolve sugar. Bring to boil, reduce heat and simmer, stirring, 3 minutes.

2. Serve warm, poured over dessert of choice (see Hints & Tips).

## HINTS & TIPS

This warm caramel sauce transforms a few simple ingredients into a divinely decadent dessert. Try one of the following combinations:

• Stir 2 sliced small bananas and 2 teaspoons brandy into sauce in pan. Continue to simmer 2 to 3 minutes until bananas are heated through. Serve over ice cream, sprinkled with chopped walnuts.
• Serve with warmed store-bought waffles and chocolate ice cream **(pictured)**.
• Serve with fresh ricotta cheese, dates and crisp wafer cookies.

# *Poached peaches with ricotta cream*

***Preparation and cooking time***
***25 minutes***

## INGREDIENTS

*2 cups (16 fl oz/500 ml) water*
*¾ cup (6 oz/180 g) sugar*
*2 medium-size ripe peaches (about 10 oz/300 g)*
*½ cup (4 oz/125 g) fresh ricotta cheese*
*2 tablespoons whipping (double) cream*
*1 tablespoon lightly packed brown sugar*

## TO MAKE

1. Combine water and sugar in saucepan and stir over low heat to dissolve sugar. Bring to boil and reduce heat to steady simmer. Add peaches and simmer 15 minutes. Remove with slotted spoon and set aside.

2. Bring syrup back to boil and boil until reduced by half, about 5 minutes.

3. Combine ricotta, cream and sugar.

4. Serve warm whole peaches with syrup and ricotta cream.

---

## HINTS & TIPS

- Use yellow or white peaches; the white ones have clinging stones but the yellow ones are usually easier to halve.
- Any remaining syrup can be used to poach more peaches next time.
- For a speedier dessert, halve peaches before poaching and reduce cooking time to 10 minutes.

# *Prunes and pears cooked in sweetened red wine*

***Preparation and cooking time 25 minutes***

## INGREDIENTS

*1 cup (8 fl oz/250 ml) red wine*
*½ cup (4 oz/125 g) sugar*
*½ cup (4 fl oz/125 ml) water*
*1 pear, peeled, halved, cored and cut into eighths*
*1 cinnamon stick*
*2 cardamom pods, crushed*
*grated zest of ½ orange*
*8 prunes*
*mascarpone or whipping (double) cream, to serve*
*wafer cookies, to serve (optional)*

## TO MAKE

1. Combine wine, sugar and water in saucepan and stir over low heat to dissolve sugar. Bring to boil and reduce heat to steady simmer.

2. Add pears, spices and orange zest and simmer 10 minutes.

3. Add prunes and cook until prunes are tender and plump, 3 to 4 more minutes. Remove fruit with slotted spoon and bring liquid back to boil. Boil until reduced by half, 3 to 4 minutes.

4. Pour syrup over pears and prunes. Serve warm with mascarpone or cream and cookies.

# Index

This edition published by Barnes & Noble, Inc.,
by arrangement with
Lansdowne Publishing Pty Ltd

1998 Barnes & Noble Books

M 10 9 8 7 6 5 4 3 2 1
ISBN 0-7607-0896-7

First published 1996
Reprinted 1997



Designer: Megan Smith
Photographer: Rowan Fotheringham
Stylist: Suzie Smith
Food Preparation: Myles Beaufort
Recipe Editor: Pat Connell

Set in Goudy on Quark Xpress
Printed in Singapore by Tien Wah Press (Pte) Ltd